FEAR OF WINNING

*A Psychologist Explores the Imposter
Syndrome in Progressive Leaders and
Explains How to Overcome It*

MICHAEL J. BADER, DMH

MICHAEL J. BADER

ISBN: 978-1-517-23947-3

FEAR OF WINNING

Our deepest fear is that we are powerful beyond measure. It is our light, not our darkness that most frightens us.

—Marianne Williamson

MICHAEL J. BADER

◆ ◆ ◆ ◆

ABOUT *FEAR OF WINNING*

"In his book *Fear of Winning*, Dr. Michael Bader addresses one of the most pernicious and widespread anxieties that leaders of all stripes, shapes, and sizes confront on all too regular a basis: the imposter syndrome. While focusing on leaders in the Progressive movement, Bader's work will help leaders in all domains understand and come to terms with this potentially derailing phenomenon. Bader's treatment of the topic is cogent, thorough, accessible and actionable. Bader is clearly passionate about the topic as well as compassionate for leaders who are dealing with its various consequences. His 8-step program for change will prove an invaluable source of help for leaders everywhere in effectively dealing with the imposter syndrome."

—Michael R. McGrath, Ph.D.
Adjunct Professor of Executive Education at the Ross School of Business, University of Michigan

MICHAEL J. BADER

♦♦♦♦

"Michael Bader is spot-on about the prevalence of the imposter syndrome in progressive leaders. In my thirty-five years of experience as a top leader of a dynamic and progressive labor union, I had occasion to see many examples of what Bader describes among the wide assortment of leaders with whom I closely worked in labor and across the progressive movement.

—Anna Burger, Co-Chair
Gettysburg Project on Civic Engagement,
retired Secretary-Treasurer of the Service
Employees International Union
Chair of Change to Win

TABLE OF CONTENTS

INTRODUCTION

his book is based on my experience treating people who are leaders—especially those from progressive political organizations—in psychotherapy over the past thirty-five years. My direct clinical experiences have been greatly supplemented by my experience consulting with and coaching leaders of progressive organizations over the past twelve years "in the field" through a group called the Institute4Change, an interdisciplinary group of experts in diverse fields that formed to help assess and develop the leadership, organization, and power of progressive political and non-profit organizations.

The I4C, as we were called, believed that insights from top practitioners in the fields of community organizing, organizational and leadership development, strategic planning, psychology, and even the dramatic arts could be combined and provide the deepest wisdom and support to leaders seeking to grow their organizations and win power in order to change the world. Ours was always an "inside/outside strategy," looking at both the psychology of leaders and the strengths and weaknesses of their organizational structures, management practices, and visions.

As a psychologist trained to help illuminate the conscious and unconscious fears and conflicts within individual leaders in order to help expand their awareness of their own psychic strengths and weaknesses and those of the people around them, my focus was on the "inside." I helped illuminate the dynamics of mental functioning for organizers and leaders, and I developed a coaching program that could be widely disseminated, aimed at supporting leaders in their personal growth.

This book, then, reflects my impressions and conclusions about the primary "issues" that tended to interfere with the optimal functioning of the courageous, hard-working leaders I both treated in my practice and coached. Whether in their work with the I4C or in their entering treatment in my consulting room, these leaders went outside their comfort zones in allowing a psychologist into their midst and their minds and I am grateful for the welcome and openness they extended to me. Their willingness to be self-reflective gave me hope about our political future.

But I also always "pressed" my work with leaders into the service of enhancing their effectiveness as political strategists, talent management leaders, and visionaries and could not have done so effectively if I, myself, didn't have the support and inspiration of my I4C teammates. I want to make special mention here of George Gates, Michael McGrath, and Ken Smith—change agents at the top of their respective games who always offered me camaraderie, support, and inspiration. I would also like to give special mention to Larry McNeil, the Director of the I4C, who mentored me about organizing, institution-building, and the hows and wherefores of building political power—and did so in ways that were always supportive and modeled the type of collaborative work we were trying to foster in the leadership teams with which we worked.

My clinical approach—the views I have about how the mind works and how it can be changed—was strongly influenced, first, by psychoanalyst Joseph Weiss, M.D. and the work about the change process that he and Harold Sampson, PhD pioneered as founders and leaders of the San Francisco Psychotherapy Research Group, and then by the work and practice of two professors at Harvard University—Robert Kegan and Lisa Lahey—whose book *Immunity to Change: How to Overcome It and Unlock the Potential in Yourself and Your Organization* and the workshops and trainings I attended that derived from their approach helped me systematize my approach to changing the beliefs and feelings that inhibited the ambitions of those leaders with whom I worked.

Since most of the clinical vignettes discussed in this book are from my clinical practice, the identities of these patients have been greatly disguised.

THE IMPOSTER SYNDROME

ost people know when they're working on a team or in an organization that's healthy and effective. They look forward to going to work. They see themselves as part of a group with a common and inspiring purpose. They expect to learn on the job and to be recognized for who they are and what they accomplish. They feel appreciated and empowered by those above them. And those above them—the leaders—feel confident that, because of their talent, hard work, and ability, they both belong at the top and are temperamentally optimistic about being able to move their organizations forward. They exude confidence and ambition. They can envision success and articulate what it takes to get there. They have the capacity to think big and long-term. Such leaders like to be surrounded by people smarter than them and devote a good portion of their time developing others in order to make themselves replaceable. As a result, the culture of these organizations privilege experimentation, self-awareness and feedback, and development.

Such organizations and their leaders are often held out and examined as "specimens" to be analyzed in books and journals that claim to have discovered the "secret sauce" behind effective leaders and organizations.

Unfortunately, while many people have tasted this sauce, few would identify it as the norm.

This is as true in progressive political organizations as in any other. Of course, when external objective conditions appear to be raining hell on institutions committed to social change, and these institutions are so chronically forced to play defense or fight and scratch to even survive, such ideals about leadership and organization can ring pretty abstract and hollow, relegated, as they too often are, to the teachings of armchair organizational consultants or university business schools.

Still, good leadership and effective organizational cultures are not so rare that leaders don't intuitively know when their own falls short of what is possible. And there is too often a large gap between what is possible and what is real. Having worked with progressive leaders for over thirty years in my clinical practice and consulted with leadership teams in the field for the last ten, I have had the up-close-and-personal experience of witnessing and helping to correct a host of psychological impediments to growth and effectiveness in organizers, teams, and leaders in progressive organizations, ranging from huge labor unions to powerful liberal think-tanks and activist non-profits.

In my experience, progressive activists and leaders usually know that they and their organizations are not performing at their capacity, not realizing their potential. But because external reality is often so complicated and noxious, they invariably focus outward and have trouble identifying internal handicaps and struggles that make defeating these external threats all the more difficult.

This book aims to help activists and leaders correct this bias, to look inward and deepen their awareness of what makes them tick on an emotional level in order to find the psychic weak spots that give rise to organizational and political dysfunctions and self-defeating practices.

MICHAEL J. BADER

The Imposter Syndrome and the Psychology of Fraudulence

I believe that the most important internal problem that causes progressive leaders to inhibit their potential and the potential for growth in their organizations is a condition known as the *Imposter Syndrome*. The Imposter Syndrome is, simply put, a collection of beliefs, usually irrational and often unconscious, that "tell" those afflicted that they're not supposed to be strong, confident, authoritative, and ambitious, lest they suffer shame, guilt, or some other type of painful psychological consequence. For example, if I believe I'm not supposed to be smart or talented and, therefore, don't deserve my position or the esteem in which I'm held, I may, as a result, be more disposed to somehow shoot myself in the foot—before someone else does.

Only by confronting, compassionately understanding, and changing these beliefs can leaders feel safe enough to free up their potential and increase the capacity of their organizations to win their battles for the power they need to change the world.

FEAR OF WINNING

There are few people I know—and none that I've treated in psychotherapy—who haven't at times felt like imposters or wrestled with feelings of fraudulence. The suffering and costs associated with such feelings are certainly familiar to many in our culture. A cursory scan of self-help books on Amazon reveals well over 200 books directly or indirectly discussing some version of the psychological harm done by feelings of fraudulence—books with titles such as *How to Stop Self-Sabotaging and Start Living*; *Inner Critics, Inner Success*; *The Imposter Syndrome*; and recently, *Lean In* by Sheryl Sandberg.

The Imposter Syndrome can afflict anyone. Yet perhaps for obvious reasons, the sense that one got where one is by mistake or subterfuge is particularly acute among people who have risen to positions of authority or leadership. It is often at the core of the emotional "baggage" leaders carry, baggage that causes unhappiness and burnout in individuals and confusion and cynicism in organizations. When these feelings infect progressive leaders, they also cripple the movement whose success depends in large part on its leaders' confidence, decisiveness, and visionary optimism. When leaders feel like frauds, a movement's sense of legitimacy and power can corrode from the inside.

The feelings of fraudulence that these leaders and activists so often experience are grounded in beliefs—sometimes unconscious, often secret—that they haven't earned what they've achieved and don't belong in the position they hold. It's as if they have been admitted to a club by mistake, a mistake that will soon be revealed, be met with disappointment, anger, or disdain, and result in a humiliating rejection or punishment—or, worse, a confirmation of the original feelings of illegitimacy.

Moreover, people who feel fraudulent often worry that others are envious of their success and secretly wish them to fail—and will relish discovering the flaw that will lead to their downfall. Such self-suspecting imposters always worry that they are one mistake away from disaster. They constantly fear being found out.

Sometimes people are so anxious about being discovered—and so sure discovery is inevitable—that they bring it on themselves to get it over with. One of my patients recently said, "I have a great husband and kids, I have a decent job, but I wake up every day telling myself that for some reason I don't deserve these good things. In fact, I find myself tempted to do things that will screw it up, although that's the opposite of what I want."

Many people also feel—despite their rational convictions to the contrary—that they're not really *supposed* to be successful or have the good things in life. Perhaps they feel guilty about having more success than their parents, extended families, those they represent, or others in their communities of origin. Having power may be inconsistent with their belief in equality; they may feel that exercising power is a betrayal of democratic ideals. Or perhaps power, success, or happiness is simply unfamiliar and therefore difficult to "own."

Emotions and the Left

Over forty years as a psychotherapist and over ten years coaching and consulting with progressive leaders more directly and formally "in the field," I have frequently seen these psychological dynamics in sharp focus and witnessed the ways they complicate and are complicated by other conflicts about dependency, helplessness, shame, and control. I've seen them deepen the depression and anxiety that seems often to accompany the human condition. I've come to understand not just the personal suffering these feelings engender but also the organizational dysfunction they may wreak.

While much has been written about the ideological, strategic, and organizational weaknesses of progressive organizations, there's been little analysis of the special ways that psychological conflicts arise in and sidetrack progressive political leaders and the institutions they serve. In fact, many leftists eschew deep psychological analysis and introspection, discounting an approach that seems to give special emphasis to internal life as soft and "touchy-feely." Just as the New Left of the 1960s rejected the psychological reductionism that translated political protests into neurotic rebellions against parental authority, so do present-day leaders feel a reflexive skepticism about psychological interpretations of their current challenges.

Of course, these reactions aren't crazy. If progressive leaders doubt themselves and worry that they may soon be found out and deposed, this is in part a rational response to laws, policies, and economic realities that *do* rob their organizations, their members, and themselves of power. If all around you the rewards and victories are going to the people who are most hostile to everything you believe in—to ruthless competitors when you are building solidarity, to enemies who will stop at nothing to defeat you when you are working for peace and justice—then it's not illogical to suspect that it's a fluke, or an error, that you are a member of any elite whatsoever. And when the world is throwing so many real and painful brickbats our way, it's no wonder many progressives think personal growth and introspection are luxuries.

In contrast, leaders in the private sector pay a great deal of attention to their inner lives. They have personal coaches. They bring in psychological consultants to help their leadership teams. They assume that healthier leaders can better create healthier organizations with healthier bottom lines. Further, private sector leaders are the beneficiaries of a huge literature aimed at helping them better understand themselves and others in order to strengthen their leadership and help them become more competitive. More books and articles have been written for corporate executives about executive coaching, the relationship between internal attitudes and external success, between emotional strength and market strength, and between unconscious self-sabotage and competitive failures, than there are leaders to read them.

I would argue that our prejudice against facing and analyzing our own internal conflicts, while understandable, is self-defeating and toxic to our avowed aims and mission. Such self-sabotage is especially tragic because it is unnecessary. There is, after all, no need to insist on a dichotomy between external and internal dysfunctions. Progressive leaders need both: psychological insight and emotional support, and also more money and better practical strategies. Both are necessary to win.

My emphasis will be on the psychological half of the problem—and what I believe is at the root of so many of the problems of leadership in our movement: that is, the *Imposter Syndrome*. This book will attempt to explain the sources and meanings of this complex of feelings and beliefs and illustrate the ways it causes trouble in both the internal *and* external worlds of many of the important participants in the struggle for a better world.

When I say that the Imposter Syndrome lies at the heart of the stress and psychological struggles of progressive leaders, I'm not implying that it is the only "syndrome" that afflicts such leaders, or that it is the only way of describing what ails them. Leaders, like all people, worry about people liking them, fear failing, are timid or hidebound in their analyses of the problems arrayed before them, become guilty if they aren't politically correct, and have trouble finding a proper work-life balance. The reason that I am risking oversimplifying the internal problems that progressives face by reducing them to issues around fraudulence is because these latter issues are so frequently seen and so often turn out to be the cause of many of the other emotional blocks that hold organizers and progressive leaders—and their organizations—back.

Someone, for example, might be so afraid of being disliked and failing that he or she becomes overly controlling and micromanages everything and everyone. The "problem" of such a person's oversensitivity to the judgments of others, however, is often really an underlying feeling of fraudulence. In such a case, a leader's expectations of negative reactions usually stem from his or her internal (and irrational) sense of legitimacy about having the authority to manage others and make decisions to begin with—a classic symptom, in other words, of the Imposter Syndrome. The fear of being disliked, then, can be best understood through the lens of this syndrome. *Thus, by reducing a large range of psychological foibles to one core conflict, I think that leaders can more clearly and simply identify the source of their self-sabotage and develop a clear and much simpler strategy for overcoming it.*

Roots of the Syndrome: Imposters are Made, not Born

Babies aren't born feeling fraudulent. They learn to feel this way about themselves in the course of growing up, in the context of family relationships. Because of the essential dependence of children on their parents or guardians, these adults have an awesome power to define for the child what *is* and what *is supposed to be*—in other words, both reality *and* morality.

Children learn about who they are through inference and direct experience in their relationships with parents and parental figures. They learn about what is legitimate to expect, how to treat others, and how other people are likely to respond to their own anger, dependence, distress, or self-assertion and independence. They learn about what it's supposed to be like to be masculine or feminine. They identify and usually comply with the role models around them.

The threat of losing a secure connection to one or both parents ensures that childhood learning becomes deeply internalized and often endures a lifetime. For example, children often feel guilty or worried about leaving their families or having more than the people they grew up with. Normal separation and success can come to feel disloyal, whether or not their families directly communicate this. These children come to believe that if they have more, then someone else will necessarily have less. They may learn that wanting or needing "too much," being assertive or just simply confident, will provoke one or both parents to feel angry, burdened, hurt, or excluded. The children develop beliefs that predict that if they feel X, the response from important others is likely to be Y. Even if X is something good or healthy—say, for example, confident self-assertion—but Y is not, then security and attachment may demand that X be inhibited or denied altogether.

Because children tend to take responsibility for much more than they should, if a child seeks more independence and becomes more self-assertive and, for even unrelated reasons, a parent is depressed, that child may conclude that the wish for autonomy is harmful and should be repressed. The result is distress and self-sabotage.

These relationships and feelings form the soil in which the imposter syndrome grows. If a child concludes that a feeling or wish threatens the adults upon whom that child is dependent, that feeling can be experienced as dangerous. When the child becomes an adult, any positive trait, accomplishment, or normal developmental aim—love, power, authority, intelligence, status, recognition, or independence—can feel undeserved, illegitimate, if that adult's childhood taught him or her that success might threaten important relationships.

If people want such things anyway (because we all do) or if their ambitions lead them into positions where it's appropriate and sanctioned to feel powerful or valued (as when they become leaders), then they can increasingly experience a psychological conflict. Healthy ambition itself becomes psychologically risky. They have something they're not supposed to have. They come to feel like imposters.

The book *Lean In* was criticized because its author, Sheryl Sandberg—the COO of Facebook—singles out the imposter syndrome as a special insecurity of successful corporate women. In fact, feelings of fraudulence *are* a special problem for women. Not only are women often held back by real-world glass ceilings, they often hold themselves back because of beliefs that confidence is a trait that belongs to men; and women will be punished as unfeminine if they presume to express it. Some of our culture's most accomplished and celebrated women—not just Sandberg but also Sonia Sotomayor, Michelle Pfeiffer, Kate Winslet, Valerie Jarrett, Maya Angelou, Oprah Winfrey, and Meryl Streep, to name just a few—have openly admitted to feelings of being an imposter. "I'd wake up in the morning before going off to a shoot and think, I can't do this," Winslet once said. "I'm a fraud."

Having said that, however, feelings of fraudulence are not exclusive to women. In fact, feelings of fraudulence span age and gender. For instance, a survey of Harvard Business School students found that seventy-five percent of both sexes believed the school had made a mistake in admitting them. Many, if not most, of the successful and powerful men I've worked with suffer from such feelings every bit as much. Men may just not be able to admit it with the same freedom as women.

The Costs of Feeling Like a Fraud

It's all well and good to name the problem of fraudulence and describe its origins and dynamics. But in order to be useful, it's vital that progressive leaders identify the specific ways that this issue might be limiting their potential and affecting their organizations and, having identified these patterns, understand that there are ways to overcome them.

The **six dysfunctional consequences of conscious and unconscious feelings of fraudulence in leaders** are:

- ➤ The paralysis of perfectionism and micro-managing

- ➤ The fear of taking risks

- ➤ The failure of self-care and the creation of a workaholic culture

- ➤ The inability to develop a learning environment that encourages creativity

- ➤ The self-defeating commitment to being the underdog

- ➤ The perpetuation of cynicism and joylessness

1. The paralysis of perfectionism and micro-managing

Suppose you were poor and snuck into an exclusive country club, pretending to be a member. You would likely be careful to observe meticulous etiquette and manners, follow the dress code exactly, and be vigilant about participating in the club's rituals in just the right way. Your desire to act like a perfect member would be the flip side of your fear of being exposed and kicked out as an illegitimate interloper. Suppose, on the other hand, you were born into wealth and your family had always belonged to that club. You could relax; take some liberties with such things as using the correct utensils or saying just the right thing to the right people. You wouldn't think for a moment that you'd be "discovered" and asked to leave. You would take for granted that you belonged.

In the first example, perfectionism is a way of not being exposed as an imposter. In the second, perfectionism is not necessary because belonging is taken for granted. Some progressive leaders feel they've snuck into their position—the "club"—and thus believe they have to be perfect to justify their presence. They fear exposure and have to guard against any negligence that might reveal the "truth." This fear and the perfectionism that results can be paralyzing.

Rita was someone I treated in psychotherapy for several years. She ran a non-profit organization with a board of directors that she felt was potentially critical of her leadership. As a result, she spent hours upon hours checking the books, balancing accounts, and making sure that all necessary reports to the board were beyond reproach. From my vantage point as her therapist, I didn't know for sure if her assumptions about the board were true or false. What I did know was that Rita felt so vulnerable to being criticized and judged that she spent way more time on the bureaucratic details of internal politics than on growing her organization, a goal that she claimed was all-important to her. Achieving such a goal was made difficult by her perpetual fear that she'd be exposed for her deficiencies.

John was the assistant director of a large union who consulted me because he knew I'd had some history working with union leaders. His job was to develop strategies to engage members more deeply in political activity. He was in charge of a team of five supervisors who were quite competent. He admitted that he checked up on their work constantly, demanding twice-weekly direct reports in person and in writing.

Although not at all my standard practice, I had an opportunity to observe one of these meetings at his work site. John questioned and gave advice to his subordinate about the smallest details, down to exact instructions about how to speak to members and mileage-saving tips on travel routes. He communicated an attitude of great worry, a worry that I knew bled into his off-hours.

Slowly burning out, John finally confessed that he simply didn't know how to stop getting "lost in the weeds." He told me that he felt responsible for everything these supervisors did, fretted that he'd be held accountable if they failed, and, if that happened, that the legitimacy of his leadership would be questioned. Coming from extremely humble origins, John sometimes doubted that he belonged in the leadership position he had clearly earned and, as a result, felt an exaggerated fear of failure.

John and Rita experienced a highly unrealistic and inappropriate sense of responsibility, even in areas they couldn't control—one of the hallmarks of feelings of fraudulence. The psychological logic was easy to see: if you are someplace or someone that you're not supposed to be, then you better make *sure* that everything is perfect and above reproach. Any reproach feels like an accusation that you don't belong or don't deserve your position. Any failure at a task is psychically equivalent to a personal failure.

A natural response under these psychological conditions will be defensiveness, anxiety, or both. The consequence can be a hyper-vigilance to details and a compulsive perfectionism that elicits resentments from staff and distracts leaders from their bigger leadership tasks. Such leaders are constantly covering their flanks when their real job is to lead their organizations forward.

When leaders micro-manage, those who are being managed begin to work defensively. They try to "stay out of trouble" when their actual job might be going out, agitating, and *creating* some trouble! They may become conservative and overly worried about not only their only mistakes but those of the people working for *them.* Everyone risks losing the forest for the trees.

Leaders should be leading, not hunting around in the weeds for land mines. In fact, those leaders who *do* sweat all the small stuff inadvertently create atmospheres in which everyone in the organization begins to do the same, subtly focusing more on not making mistakes and covering their tracks if they do, rather than taking initiative. When an organization is overly worried about small things, it usually can't do big things.

2. The failure to take risks

Perfectionists—those overly worried about making mistakes and being exposed as frauds—are, by nature, risk-averse. At some point, leaders need to take risks. Civil rights leaders pursued a risky strategy of civil disobedience. Union leaders sometimes press their members to strike. A liberal environmental organization may take a more radical stance against corporate power. A church leader comes out in favor of gay marriage. The leaders of a women's organization hitherto focused on reproductive rights chooses to expand its platform to emphasize economic inequality.

Naturally, such risks are preceded by a great deal of analysis and planning. But our movement depends on leaders' ability to, at some point, take a leap, unsure of where they will land, to put themselves and their organizations on the line in the service of getting bigger and gaining power.

Leaders who feel fraudulent in their positions are rarely able to do this. They are risk averse due to two interrelated fears. First, they feel uncomfortable being seen as bold decision-makers. And second, they fear that any real or perceived failure will be their just desserts for having the hubris to act boldly—as confirmation, in other words, that they don't deserve the authority to take organizational risks to begin with.

The Director of a progressive and well-respected planning agency in a large East Coast city had risen up in his organization by, in part, muting his more radical beliefs and instincts. However, he revealed that he was currently in active conversations with his staff about putting a proposition on the ballot in an upcoming general election that would effectively municipalize a utility that had long been overcharging city residents. He feared that, if he used the political capital he'd gained over the years (by presenting a more moderate version of his politics), he would now incur the wrath of business interests on his Board of Directors and be fired. Strategically, he felt sure that this was the time to act and that the aforementioned proposition had a good chance of passing. But, just below the surface, he questioned his right to boldly make his case to his Board and others and push for something rooted in his passion, intellect, and political ideals. Too risky, he told me.

This patient saw himself as stepping off the edge of a building and risking everything.

"Who do I think I am?" he worried aloud to me. "The Board will feel that I've been deceiving them all this time and punish me for it."

"Perhaps you could just try to think of yourself as you really are—the smartest guy in the room and one with the highest ideals and vision," I offered.

"Why should someone be punished for thinking and acting big?"

He calmed down and, in fact, moved ahead with his plan. His Board *did* react negatively and withhold their approval but told him that they appreciated his taking initiative.

Leadership means stepping out and taking risks. Sometimes leaders have to make unpopular decisions or decisions that push back against organizational inertia, partners' resistance, or enemies' hostility. The leaders can try to build internal consensus and buy-in from allies, but sometimes this is impossible; they must act. When the thought of such public assertion of authority triggers fraudulence fears, the impulse is to pull back and play it safe. They, their organizations, and the movements to which those organizations are committed pay the price.

A Local union leader in the building trades became convinced that his staff had become overly focused on handling grievances and had failed to develop enough meaningful relationships with their members. He had a plan that he was anxious about implementing: He would instruct his field staff to cease all grievance handling for three months and, instead, do nothing but have individual meetings with ordinary members—not simply the discontented ones—and get to know them better as people without asking them to do anything or help the union in any way at the end of the conversation. The aim of these meetings would be non-instrumental, aiming instead only to form and deepen relationships.

He expected push-back from his staff and disapproval from his superiors at the International. At the heart of the matter, however, was his discomfort about acting bold and self-confident, communicating to those below and above that he *knew what he was doing* and that a radical change was needed. He felt paralyzed.

"What if it didn't work" he asked?

"Well, you've been telling me that your Local is shrinking," I replied. "What do you have to lose?"

The answer, we discovered couldn't be found in some set of feared external consequence, but the internal consequence of feeling guilty and ashamed at "getting ahead of other leaders" in his union and being attacked as a result. I told him that he believed, at some level, that he wasn't supposed to be more inspired and inspiring than others; a legacy of his childhood, not his real experience in his union.

He went ahead and implemented his plan. Organizers reported enormous excitement among their members whom they had gotten to know better in one meeting than they had in ten years of relating to them exclusively around grievances. Union membership stabilized and turnout in the next general election increased substantially.

3. The failure of self-care and the creation of a workaholic culture

People who feel like imposters tend to neglect their own needs. If they've achieved any degree of success, "excessive" self-care seems especially self-indulgent and risky. Leaders on the political Left feel particularly undeserving of the help, service, support, deference, or any of a number of "perks" that our culture affords those who are powerful, successful, or otherwise important. They are supposed to be champions of the underdog, those victims of inequalities who are trapped and held back by an oppressive social system. So the champions of the poor are uncomfortable about paying themselves too much, taking care of their own needs for leisure and pleasure, or expecting others to defer to and serve their interests. Who are they to be worthy of these things?

The logic—or illogic, I should say—goes: "I shouldn't expect or take more for myself than the people whom I'm trying to help or serve." And that "more" includes the wide range of self-care activities necessary to doing a good job at serving those people. Over and over, we've seen leaders burn out, take their smartphones on vacation so as to be available 24/7, and fail to afford themselves time to reflect on their jobs and their lives.

In working with one organization around issues of time-management, my colleagues and I made the argument that the *first* thing a leader should do when scheduling the week is to block out personal and reflection time. Everyone agreed and promised to move in this direction during the next week. Several people returned excited at the progress they'd made. One person proudly stood up and said that he had succeeded in letting his phone ring four times before answering it. Another announced that she had stood her ground: during a four-day vacation, she had set a limit and did not participate in her team's obligatory 7 a.m. senior staff meeting! One small step for the individual; one even smaller step for their organizations.

In fact, failures of self-care radiate throughout an organization. Over and over, leaders report that their organizations are unable to retain young people precisely for this reason. Marriages were on the rocks. Kids were acting out because of parental absence. Health conditions were worsening, obesity increasing.

Feelings of fraudulence were invariably an important underlying dynamic force in these cultures. We heard many people express guilt and worry if they dared privilege their own needs over the needs of their clients, members, or contributors. They feared, sometimes correctly, that their peers would see such ordinary benefits as vacations, sick leave, or reasonable work hours as indicators of an absence of true commitment to "the cause." Equally compelling, they wondered if their own professed commitment was fraudulent, and that treating themselves kindly was proof.

For leaders like these, the only way to prove they are not fakers or slackers is to behave like martyrs—and force their staff to be martyrs, too, by creating cultures of sacrifice and workaholism. One of the reasons that many organizers eventually left the United Farm Workers Union was that UFW President Cesar Chavez paid them so little and expected them to work and feel compensated by their "mission." This was a dysfunctional leadership "style." People don't admire, or want to work with, martyrs who deprive themselves.

An important but little-discussed byproduct of the workaholic culture often found in progressive organizations is the relatively high incidence of alcoholism or drug addiction in leaders and organizers. Alcohol and drugs are ways to numb or escape stress, and too often the stereotype of hard drinking union "bosses" reflects a tragic truth: When people feel responsible for and obligated to others, feelings bordering on omnipotence, internal life comes to feel like a pressure cooker, one readily alleviated by trips to the bar, tranquilizers, or sleeping pills. In my ten years of consulting with unions and activist non-profits, scarcely an evening went by that wasn't brought to an end in a local hotel bar.

Martyrdom does not prove genuine commitment to a progressive movement. After all, the point of our movement is to guarantee a good life for everyone. True leaders value themselves and their staff enough to make sure everyone is competitively paid and to create workplaces that allow and encourage time and freedom for leisure, pleasure, health, and reflection.

4. The inability to create a learning environment that encourages creativity

Fears of fraudulence prevent leaders from honoring their own personal and professional development and produce organizations that stifle creativity. When leaders are blocked in their own growth, they build environments in which providing service and "doing the job" become the only norms that are valued and recognized.

I have worked with many progressive leaders on creating "personal development plans." These are formal sets of steps leading to goals that both the leader and I agree would be personally gratifying, represent professional growth, and directly or indirectly enhance the person's capacity to contribute to the growth of his or her organization. Leaders generally start out enthusiastic about the possibility that they could privilege their own developmental needs and interests, as well as create a culture of learning in their organizations. In each and every case, despite an initial excitement and verbal buy-in, these leaders found ways to procrastinate about—or avoid altogether—the learning process that everyone had agreed was critically important.

A small example will illustrate this point. A leader of an important progressive organization—I'll call him Roger—came into therapy with me wanting to sharpen and more aggressively pursue his ambitions, including crafting a personal development plan. He told me that he had been tremendously impressed by a political autobiography written by an important player in both Clinton administrations. One of Roger's colleagues knew this individual well; the colleague told my patient that the writer was still active in politics and would, given Roger's current prominence, likely jump at the chance to develop a closer relationship with Roger. However, Roger became exceedingly anxious about the prospect of direct contact with the author he admired so much. He protested, "But I'd have nothing to say!" On the face of it, this was absurd. But Roger felt like an imposter who had nothing of value to bring to the table. Despite our best efforts, Roger never made the connection he so eagerly desired.

I came to understand that one of the core sources of this resistance was leaders' belief that they were imposters: On one hand, their own learning and growth did not deserve to be given priority. On the other, if they tried to grow, they might just fail. The goal of being bigger and better was—while embraced publicly—privately feared and inhibited.

There is another, somewhat less common, manifestation of a leader's inability to create a learning environment due to feelings of fraudulence. It is not rare for someone who is uneducated, or who feels undereducated, to assume a position of responsibility and power in an organization, particularly if that organization tries to raise its worker-members to leadership. Although not limited to one sub-group, this situation may often involve people who come from poverty or have been victims of discrimination and who have gone on to become self-educated.

One manifestation of an imposter syndrome in these cases is a tendency to speak in abstractions rather than concretely, using highly intellectual rather than everyday language. It's as if this language were a secret incantation granting entry to an exclusive club that was otherwise fraudulently given. Along with talking "up" is a tendency to look down on other staff, to be unable to let them be smarter than the leader or to help them develop qualities valued in the organization.

Good leaders don't have to be "the smartest person in the room." They check their own egos— whether overly healthy or in need of much care and feeding—at the door. The job of a great leader is to provide the conditions and encouragement under which others can be better. To leaders who are constantly proving that they belong through exaggerated displays of intellect, such a supportive role is anathema.

5. The self-defeating commitment to being an underdog

Progressive leaders often run the risk of moving from empathizing to over-identifying with the underdog. Empathy is different than identification. Empathy is like a trial identification. One temporarily puts oneself in someone else's shoes and experiences some version of what that other person feels. Empathy is the bread and butter of psychotherapy, of course; but it is also a valuable trait for progressive leaders. The plight of those victimized in our society isn't an abstraction. If the leader can feel some of their pain, the result is a greater and more passionate determination to relieve their suffering.

We all know people who lack empathy—for instance, politicians who talk about poverty or injustice as if such afflictions were talking points on a campaign cheat sheet. But we've also seen elected leaders occasionally display genuine empathy—say, President Bill Clinton addressing local students and faculty with deep feeling after the Columbine school shooting, or even New York City Mayor Rudy Giuliani for moments immediately after 9/11.

But while empathizing with victims is good, over-identifying with them is not. Over-identification with the victim involves a false and exaggerated *denial of difference.* The leaders and staff of progressive organizations are usually *not* in the exact same boat as the victims of an exploitative and unfair social order. Leaders generally make decent incomes, have housing, cars, vacations, sick leave, and status. Their kids go to decent schools; they do not fear a free fall into poverty when they retire. They do not feel completely helpless and powerless. Progressive leaders are socially, emotionally, and often physically healthier than the people they work to help. The differences may be relative, but they're real.

There is no reason for leaders to try to disguise the experience, learning, and hard work that got them where they are and try to be "one of the people." After all, you want your doctor to know more about medicine than you do; it's not helpful or reassuring for a patient to be asked, "Well, what do you want to do?" without any facts or guidance. Just as African-Americans often feel a private disdain for white liberals trying to talk "street" or "ghetto," so do most of the people we want to organize distrust organizers who pander by making themselves out to be someone they're not.

Again, this trust-killing masquerade is rooted in progressive leaders' feelings of guilt and fraudulence. Too often, they imagine that if they do not hide or play down the talent, power, status, and other good things in their lives, they'll be resented, envied, and punished by those who have less. The leaders might then over-identify with the victim as a defense against what they *imagine* to be the latter's envy and resentment. Progressive leaders are sometimes so driven to *not* be seen as oppressors that they exaggerate the extent that they're victims.

People can tell the difference between authentic empathy and a pretense of "sameness." They are more eager to collaborate with staff and leaders who are confident, optimistic, ambitious, and make no bones about being talented. Such progressive leaders, in turn, discredit themselves by putting themselves down when they over-identify with the victim, pretending that they are worse off than they are, depriving themselves of satisfactions that their station in life affords, unable to lead because guilt and feelings of fraudulence invalidate the conviction that they are *necessary* to the project's success.

Ernest described spending years organizing ministers in East Los Angeles, most of them African-American. He described being excoriated by these ministers for his alleged presumption that they needed help from him, a white outsider. Finally,

Ernest felt enough mutual trust to say, "Well, look around you. What the hell have *you* done to change the dynamics in your community? Looks pretty dismal to me!" This was the turning point in a process that led to a productive collaboration. Such an intervention certainly required that the white organizer have empathy, but he also needed to resist surrendering to unfair critiques and let himself own the experience, education, talent, and even relative comfort that made him equal to the task at hand.

Successful leaders empathize with and respect—but also accept unapologetically their difference from—those who may be less fortunate than they. Fully accepting their own assets will allow them to accomplish, alongside the people they are working with, what those people have been unable to accomplish on their own. In other words, good leaders must resist feeling guilty about their relative privilege or fraudulent about their personal gifts.

6. The perpetuation of cynicism and joylessness

No organization can prosper without a compelling vision. "A compelling vision pulls, animates, energizes," said Larry McNeil, an experienced organizer and colleague. "It fulfills the basic human need to be about something bigger than ourselves, to free us up from the jail of always living in the present tense." This jail that McNeil refers to is, in part, the jail of cynicism. It is the belief that the way things are is the way they're supposed to be, that—despite proclamations to the contrary—the present is the best predictor of the future.

The jail of living always in the present ultimately serves the purpose of safety. You don't have to put anything on the line, risk public failures, or be accused of overreaching. This type of stasis is a consequence of feelings of fraudulence. If imposters have to play it safe, they can't be active and aggressive change agents. They can't shoot too high. They can't conduct themselves in a free and easy way—as if they belong where they are. Their idealism is thin, belied by a much more solid foundation of cynicism.

Cynicism masquerades as political savvy. It calls itself "realism" because its opposite—passionate idealism—leaves the cynic too vulnerable to shame, accusations of naiveté, and the belittling attacks by those "in the know" who are always choosing between the lesser of two evils so as not to reach for what they truly believe is good, and fail.

Cynicism—which takes elements of reality and weaves them into an unconsciously conservative worldview—is also the haven of self-perceived imposters. If they do nothing but follow received, inherently cynical wisdom, no one can accuse them of hubris, of making illegitimate claims to leadership and power, of being grandiose or, worse, *unrealistic.* If they accomplish what conservatism always aims to accomplish—that is, as little as possible—their cynical prophecy has been realized. They have, at least for the moment, proven themselves to be part of the club of those "in the know"—those who know that very little changes because very little *can* change.

Self-protective cynicism has another toxic effect on people and organizations. Holding ourselves back from enthusiasm, excitement, or passion in order to avoid looking naïve or foolish in the eyes of our peers, we drain the joy out of our work and our workplaces.

Leaders' compulsion to keep doing what they've always done, even if it does not work, is rooted in their fears of being discredited and losing their status and power if they break the mold and shoot too high. In other words, the Imposter

Syndrome, in practice, is a practice of cynicism. After all, who are they to be so bold? Who are they to defy the conventional wisdom parroted by those other, *legitimate* leaders? By extension, how could the organization they lead presume to make a real difference? The voice of cynicism is putting this poisonous message in these leaders' ears: Where does your organization, your social movement, get the chutzpah to change the world?

And, yet, it's believing in and collectively striving for ideals that make political work feel good; shooting high for something that is inspiring generates energy and joy. Playing it safe dampens spirits, even if it also insures a certain type of safety. People have a need to connect with something bigger and better than themselves, something with a grander significance, and when they hear their leaders articulate such a vision, they don't feel resentment or envy but pride and a sense of being uplifted.

Leaders doing the inspiring need to understand and internalize this basic fact: Setting the bar high and overcoming the safety of cynicism infuses oneself and one's organization with a passion sorely lacking today in many of our organizations.

OVERCOMING THE IMPOSTER SYNDROME

here is a saying in 12-step groups that goes, "Fake it 'til you make it." It is meant to convey that sometimes emotions follow actions, that *acting* in a clean and sober way can generate positive experiences that lessen the belief that getting high is the only way to feel good.

Put another way, if you expect to be shamed or punished for pursuing a bold goal or expressing an important ambition, those expectations can prevent you from trying to achieve it. But if you act anyway, move forward in the face of fear and self-doubt, you may gradually discover that the dreaded outcome is nowhere to be found. I've treated many leaders who began their jobs feeling like imposters. Then, over the years, experiences accrue that reinforce their confidence in their abilities and their sense of legitimacy. They no longer feel like imposters.

It is a special kind of learning. Irrational beliefs underlying feelings of fraudulence begin to weaken, allowing more and bolder forms of experimentation until that voice saying "You're an imposter" diminishes to a whisper.

Not everyone who struggles with feelings of fraudulence needs therapy or coaching. Positive experience itself can promote growth. Sometimes, however, naturally occurring experience doesn't do the job. People in the grips of a deep-seated belief and fear have a hard time changing. They may get positive affirming feedback from others, but selectively read it as phony or secretly believe that they've tricked others into giving it. Or they give excessive weight to the opinion of even one person among many who confirms their self-doubt. In such cases, more aggressive therapeutic interventions may be called for.

The personal and organizational emotional work may last a month or several years. It may happen in a group of peers or with a psychotherapist or coach (I use the terms therapist and coach here interchangeably). Every person is different; the process has to be sensitively tailored to the needs of the person being coached. But even though in the section that follows I address "you," I don't believe that these changes can be made alone.

The "Eight-Step Program" for Change

Here are the broad outlines of the steps I've applied in helping many, many leaders to understand and overcome their crippling feelings of fraudulence. These steps are not just about you, the individual, though; nor about your private sense of wellbeing. They are about constructing a vision, for yourself and your organization, mapping the fears and doubts that cloud it, and then clearing those clouds away in order to see and achieve success. I've not only seen this model generate tremendous results in the work I do in my office but have been profoundly influenced by very similar work done in groups and organizations by Robert Kegan and Lisa Lahey, authors of a groundbreaking book, *Immunity to Change: How to Overcome It and Unlock the Potential in Yourself and Your Organization*, in much larger contexts. I liberally—and frequently—draw on their brilliant model here.

I'll illustrate this "eight-step program" with the story of Hector, a Hispanic man who came from humble origins and rose to become the powerful chief of staff of a large labor union. Still, in some secret place in his heart, Hector did not believe he belonged there. He felt like an imposter. Only vanquishing that feeling would free Hector to do what he was capable of in leading his union to its fullest potential.

1. Identify the most important and passionately held goal.

What is the thing you *most* want to get better at and that your organization most *needs* you to get better at? Hector was passionately committed to his union and its members and to the large movement for social justice of which it was a part. But day-to-day he seemed to be doing nothing to advance any of that. So for himself, he wanted to learn let go of the small stuff and carve out the time and acquire the psychological freedom to reflect on the long-term future of the organization it was his responsibility and privilege to lead. Only then, he felt, could he help unlock the union's potential power.

Hector's problem, as he described it to me, was that he repeatedly found himself immersed in trivia or micro-managing rather than working on and beginning to implement a strategic vision for his organization. He knew he had to pull back from the day-to-day operations of his organization to be able to feel and act bigger, to—as he described this aspiration—"play with the big boys." His vision was to lead his union to grow, gain power, and change the lives of its members and other workers for the better. But he did not really believe he was, or even deserved to be, one of the "big boys." Feelings of fraudulence held him back.

2. Take a ruthless inventory of the behaviors that systematically impede achieving these big goals.

Kegan and Lahey suggest that, having identified your most important goals, you "tell on yourself" by listing the behaviors that interfere with making progress toward those goals. Hector admitted that he was constantly worrying about whether his staff members were doing their jobs. He required them to submit frequent reports describing work that they most likely were able to handle independently. He carried these worries home and would call people he supervised in the evening and on weekends to check up on them.

Meanwhile, he spent almost no time or energy imagining what kind of help *he* might need to develop as a leader, who *he* might have to form relationships with to multiply the power of his organization, and how *he* might put the right people in the right positions to give him the freedom to lead.

3. Imagine what it would feel were these obstacles suddenly, magically to disappear.

Kegan and Lahey, echoing the experience of good clinicians everywhere, underline the crucial value—but also difficulty—of this next step. We ask the client to look inside and try to sense a feeling of distress or discomfort that might begin to arise if he or she visualizes success.

"I'd feel great," Hector answered immediately when I put this challenge to him. Then we dug deeper. I asked him to try to detect, somewhere inside his non-rational mind, *any* reluctance, worry, or conflict that might emerge if he were to radically eliminate the dysfunctional habits of a lifetime. Both for Kegan and Lahey and in my own clinical practice, this question gets to the heart of the matter. Self-defeating behaviors and inhibitions are ultimately based on fears. Bringing them to the surface is the key to freeing oneself of them. And, in the process, I invariably see the footprints of some version of an Imposter Syndrome.

What were Hector's worst fantasies?

Admitting to such fantasies can be embarrassing. In the light of day they look ridiculous—and contradict the avowed ambition to change for the better. But at their heart is the fear of fraudulence and the belief that if you really got out of your own way, became the leader you wanted to be, really grew into your best self, you would be exposed as an imposter and suffer intolerable feelings of loss, rejection, and failure.

Hector imagined people thinking or even saying things like, "Who is he to be acting like such a big shot? He's a nobody who is pretending to be a somebody!" While he knew this was an irrational fear, he also came to see that it was, indeed, one that he believed deep down might happen, and he felt a taste of the humiliation that would accompany it.

"No wonder you have mixed feelings about acting like the leader you really are, Hector," I said. "Look at what you fear might happen!"

4. Uncover the sources of the fear.

Now you have named the fear and negative beliefs and imagined life without them. The next step is exploring and reconstructing their sources. Almost invariably, the feeling of being an imposter was born in childhood. It is an axiom in my coaching and psychotherapy work that, in order to move forward, one often has to reconstruct one's past.

Together, Hector and I explored the childhood roots of his obsessive worries about the work that others could and, if allowed and encourage to, would be taking care of. We discovered that he felt enormous survivor guilt for having achieved so much more in life than anyone in his family or community. He worried that his current leadership position was tenuous: if everything were not perfect, he'd be found out, shamed, and taken down. So he felt safer playing defense, shoring up the status quo, even at the costs of feeling disappointed in himself, the happiness and productivity of his staff, and the health and effectiveness of the entire organization.

5. Share these conflicts and fears. Ask for help.

Identify one or more trusted friends or colleagues in your workplace. These allies can give immediate feedback after a meeting, action, or project about whether or not your worst fears came true.

Hector screwed up his courage to announce to his senior leadership team his intention to "let go" of much of the day-to-day operations of the organization. He identified two people he trusted who could give him feedback as to whether, in each meeting they attended together, his "worst" fears about the judgment of others were actually realized. Invariably, they were not. Armed with such real-time feedback, Hector felt safer—little by little—to become even bolder.

6. Identify situations in which to try out new behaviors—and try them out.

Take actions you've identified as laden with the potential for exposure and shame—but also with the potential for great success. Start with low-risk experiments and build up from there.

For Hector, the first try-out was simply meeting with his direct reports less frequently. He simply changed his schedule. Then he began to hold people more accountable. Next, he began to talk more with his senior team about his strategic vision for the future and made it clearer and clearer that this was the direction he wanted to take.

He hired someone whose sole job was to arrange meetings with power brokers and funders in his state. Finally, Hector gave himself what he had never felt he deserved. He made Friday afternoon a sacrosanct time, without meetings or other obligations, in which he could read, think, and write about where he wanted the organization to go.

7. Learn not just from your failures but also from your successes.

Change, by definition, is a process of trial and— the thing the self-identified imposter fears most— error.

Each step along Hector's way was accompanied by renewed anxiety about overstepping his bounds, risking failure, and being exposed as a fraud. Each time, we tried to find ways of helping him check out his expectations, sometimes by asking people and other times by more clearly seeing how his past was being repeated in his present. And still other times, we talked about his distorted and irrational fears of the dangers of making mistakes and of the punishment he would endure for having the hubris to take risks that invariably included imperfections in planning and execution.

Gradually, Hector began to have successes. He began to slowly set up meetings with power brokers in his state and got special coaching in order to develop a more inspiring media presence. Each success weakened his worries about being a fraud. Each propelled him to take on bigger and more ambitious projects. Success fed on success. He began to realize he was not just one of the "big boys." He was the right person for this job—the job of leadership.

8. Spread the wealth.

One of the greatest benefits of personal change of the sort described above is that a top leader can then slowly begin to influence the culture of the organization to support these types of changes in others. Throwing off the cloak of the "imposter" allows the leader to see the real talents and enthusiasm of his staff.

Hector eventually required each member of his senior leadership team also to have a "coach." People were encouraged to talk to each other about the changes they were working on and the fears they were trying to overcome. Such conversations became more "normal" and, since the organization was becoming healthier and more effective, no longer seemed like distractions from the "real" work of senior leadership but an integral part of it.

When a culture changes, some people resist and resent it; some even have to leave. Others find themselves challenged in productive ways. And still others come to see themselves and others in entirely new ways—ways that enable them to do things they may never have imagined they could.

MICHAEL J. BADER

The Challenge of Authenticity

Psychological change for its own sake is good. But when such change is yoked to the personal aspirations of leaders to be better and stronger *leaders,* the results pay off in political ways, as well.

When the leaders of an organization find their own strengths and let go of the fears that narrow their imagination and stanch their courage, the other people in their organization and the organization as a whole become stronger and more resilient. The organization grows less anxious about taking risks and shooting high, less uncomfortable about seeking, acquiring, and using power. It becomes more relevant to the project of progressive change.

There is no rational reason for leaders to be scared of change, although there are a host of irrational ones. One of the most important responsibilities that leaders have is to use all the internal and external resources at their command to distinguish between the two.

The choice for progressive leaders is plain: Are they going to allow themselves to continue to behave like the imposters they fear they are, and in so doing, prove that they are not the leaders they are capable of being?

Or will they allow themselves to take the risks of looking foolish or naïve, the risks of trying and failing, in order to build a movement that has the power to fashion a radically better future?

◆ ◆ ◆ ◆

ABOUT THE AUTHOR

ichael Bader, DMH is a licensed psychologist and psychoanalyst currently practicing in San Francisco. In 2002, he was one of the founders of the *Institute4Change*. He has treated, coached, and taught hundreds of leaders in the progressive community, bringing insights from his clinical practice to bear on problems of leadership and organizational change. He not only received extensive training in psychotherapy and psychoanalysis in San Francisco but found additional training with Robert Kegan and Lisa Lahey in their *Minds at Work* program in Cambridge, Massachusetts.

Dr. Bader has written extensively in his own field of psychology and has also pioneered studies looking at the intersection of psychology, culture, and politics. He has published three books and over sixty articles on these topics in print magazines, edited collections, academic journals, and popular websites such as *Alternet*.org and *HuffingtonPost.com*.

A list of his publications can be found on his website: *www.michaelbader.com*.

He currently splits his time between San Francisco and Grass Valley, California.